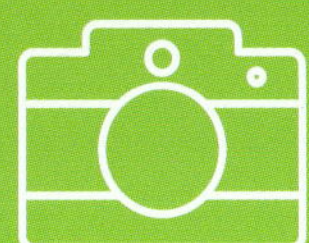

THE BEST EVER JOBS

JOBS IN ART

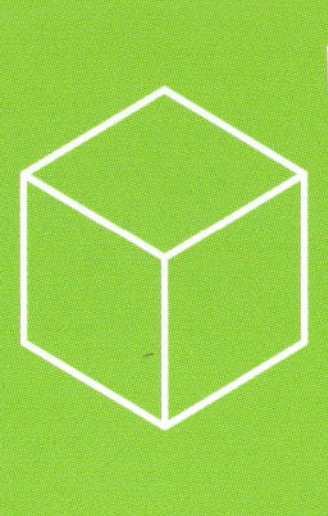

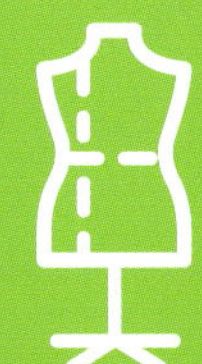

ROB COLSON

PowerKiDS press.

NEW YORK

Published in 2023 by The Rosen Publishing Group, Inc.
29 East 21st Street, New York, NY 10010

Series editor: Amy Pimperton
Produced by Tall Tree Ltd
Editor: Lara Murphy
Designer: Gary Hyde

Cataloging-in-Publication Data

Names: Colson, Rob.
Title: Jobs in art / Rob Colson.
Description: New York : PowerKids Press, 2023. | Series: The best ever jobs | Includes glossary and index.
Identifiers: ISBN 9781725339101 (pbk.) | ISBN 9781725339118 (library bound) | ISBN 9781725339125 (ebook)
Subjects: LCSH: Art--Vocational guidance--Juvenile literature
Classification: LCC N8350.C647 2023 | DDC 702.3--dc23

Picture Credits
t-top, b-bottom, l-left, r-right, c-centre, fc-front cover, bc-back cover
3t, 3br, 41t and 44b shutterstock/balabolka, 3tr and 32r shutterstock/GIN48, 3cr, 26r and 27l shutterstock/Shorena Tedliashvili, 3b and 20bl shutterstock/sinoptic, 4bl shutterstock/Kudryashka, 5tr shutterstock/om_illustrations, 5cl shutterstock/Xana_UKR, 5cr shutterstock/Laura Reyero, 5b shutterstock/Mark Rademaker, 6b shutterstock/In-Finity, 7t shutterstock/Denis Makarenko, 7cl shutterstock/enjoy your life, 8b shutterstock/TopVectorElements, 9t getty/Jemal Countess/Stringer, 9cl shutterstock/Alex Pin, 9b shutterstock/Oxy_gen, 10c shutterstock/Mochipet, 11t shutterstock/zixia, 11b shutterstock/Kathy Hutchins, 12c shutterstock/frantic00, 13t shutterstock/Sergiy Palamarchuk, 13r shutterstock/Adisa, 14b shutterstock/AVD_88, 15tr shutterstock/primiaou, 15cr shutterstock/samui, 15b shutterstock/andersphoto, 16b shutterstock/alinabel, 17t and 19t shutterstock/Featureflash Photo Agency, 17c and 17b shutterstock/godfather744431, 18b shutterstock/DOCTOR BLACK, 19b shutterstock/SunshineVector, 20tr shutterstock/Ondrej Prosicky, 21b Rondal Partridge, 22b shutterstock/ivan_kislitsin, 23t shutterstock/FashionStock.com, 23b shutterstock/Gorodenkoff, 24b shutterstock/Aluna1, 25t Carlo Maratta, 25b shutterstock/Monika Pa, 27b Bbudis/Frederico Mendes, 28b and 48b shutterstock/vi73, 29t shutterstock/andersphoto, 29b shutterstock/all_is_magic, 30-31 Herman Miller, 33t shutterstock Leonard Zhukovsky, 33b shutterstock/Aluna 1, 34b shutterstock/Aleksandr Artt, 35t shutterstock/tiny selena, 35b shutterstock/Markus Wissmann, 36l shutterstock/Maria Kazanova, 36c shutterstock/Gate Out, 36r shutterstock/Maria Kazanova, 36bl shutterstock/Kluva, 37t shutterstock/Olga Strelnikova, 37b Flickr/Amber Gregory, 38bl shutterstock/Luciano Mortula – LGM, 39t shutterstock/JuliusKielaitis, 39b shutterstock/Romain Biard, 40b shutterstock/Sunwand24, 41b Alamy Stock Photo/Keith Larby, 42b shutterstock/Everett – Art, 43t shutterstock/Shutterstaken, 43b shutterstock, 45t Swilts, 45b rohnjones.

Manufactured in the United States of America

CPSIA Compliance Information: Batch #CSPK23. For further information contact Rosen Publishing, New York, New York at 1-800-237-9932.

Find us on 

Contents

Top art jobs 4
Animator 6
Set designer 8
Special effects artist 10
Behind the scenes: Film set 12
Interior designer 14
Stylist 16
Fashion designer 18
Photographer 20
Behind the scenes: Fashion shoot 22
Landscape architect 24
Jewelry designer 26
Product designer 28
Behind the scenes: Herman Miller 30
Graphic designer 32
Illustrator 34
Art director 36
Behind the scenes: Designing a brand 38
Fine artist 40
Behind the scenes: Restoring *The Night Watch* 42
Art therapist 44

Glossary 46

Index 48

Top art jobs

Is art your favorite subject at school? Do you spend your free time doodling designs? You can put that creativity to use in a wide range of exciting jobs, creating stylish looks for the world we live in. You might become a designer, making the clothes we wear, the furniture we use, or the posters we see. Or you might use your art skills to create animated films or TV shows. Artists make their mark in lots of different ways.

ANCIENT ARTISTS

As an artist, you are doing something that people have done for tens of thousands of years. Ancient designers created clothing and jewelry from materials they found around them, including brightly colored stones or the skins of the animals they hunted. Ancient painters created images of animals and people on cave walls. Art brings pleasure to people's lives, and with today's technology, there are more ways for us to express ourselves than ever before.

Ancient artists used natural materials, such as soot, to create cave paintings.

PRACTICAL SKILLS

Making art requires lots of practical skills. Today, many artists and designers work mostly on computers, while others use traditional skills, such as carpentry or glassmaking, to craft objects. You'll need to pay close attention to the details and put in hours of practice to perfect your skills. You will also need knowledge from other STEAM subjects to create your art, such as math and science.

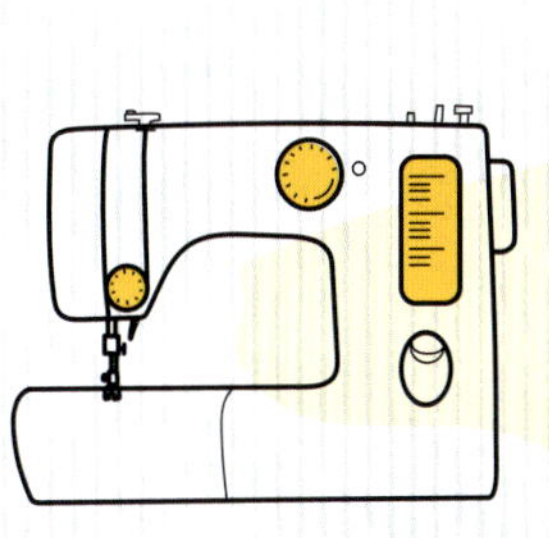

ART COLLEGE

Often, the first step to a career in the visual arts is an art degree at college. You'll get to try your hand at lots of different kinds of art, from painting and sculpture to filmmaking and graphic design. You will also learn the theory and history of art and design and study subjects such as color theory, or how to combine colors to the best effect. At the end of your studies, you get to display your work to the public at a show.

Animator

Are you a big fan of comic books and storytelling? Animators tell stories with moving pictures. They create animations and visual effects for everything from film and TV to video games and smartphone apps. You will work closely with writers, directors, and actors to develop characters and storylines that bring your ideas to life.

STORYBOARDS

Storyboard artists work with directors to turn the words in a script into images. A storyboard is a series of comic-strip images that tell a visual story. Once finished, the artist presents the storyboard to a creative team and talks them through each image. This is the stage where any problems with the script can be fixed before the film or game is made. Storyboard artists also play an important role in developing the final look and feel of the animation.

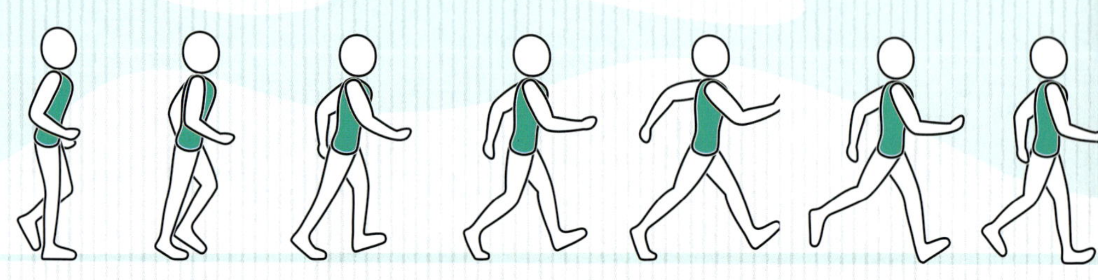

STEAM STAR:
HAYAO MIYAZAKI
(1941-)

Japanese animator and director Hayao Miyazaki has made a series of award-winning animated feature films, including the Oscar-winning *Spirited Away*, about a young girl who enters a world of ghosts to free her parents from a wicked witch. Miyazaki uses a mix of hand-drawn images and computer animation to create a rich visual style for his films, which are often set in fantasy worlds.

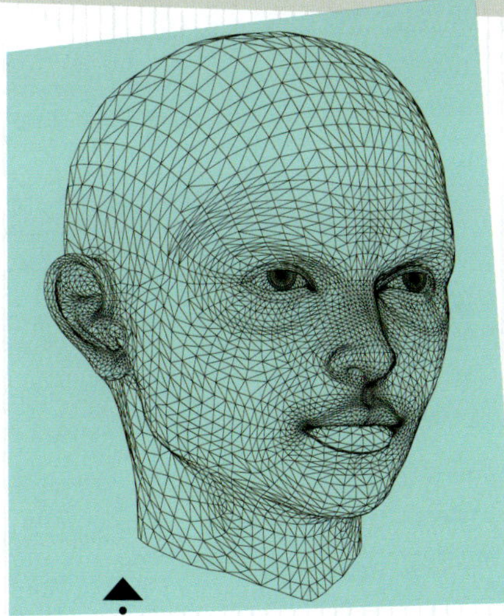

A 3D computer model of a human head

3D MODELING

Most animation today is made using computers. 3D modelers create animated creatures that look solid. Often these creatures will interact with live actors in the finished film. To bring your creatures to life, you'll need a great understanding of biomechanics—the study of the way bodies move. Often 3D modelers copy the actions of real creatures to make their creations more believable and sometimes as scary as possible!

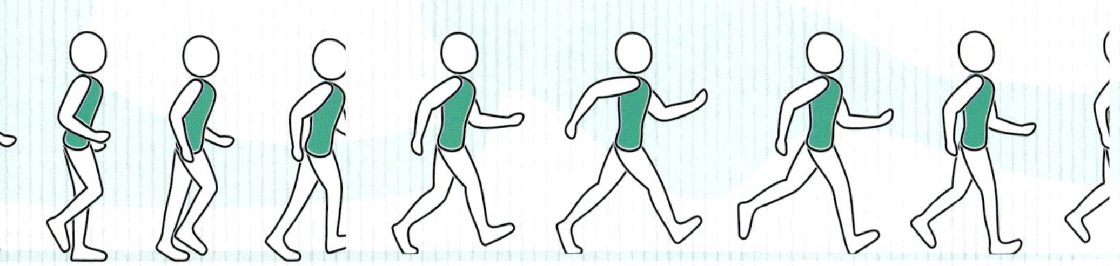

Set designer

Do you enjoy working with your hands and making things? Set designers plan and build the sets for film, TV, and the theater. Working closely with the director, the set designer is responsible for creating the look and atmosphere of the production. You'll need to be highly imaginative to come up with exciting solutions on a tight budget and be prepared to work with very tight deadlines.

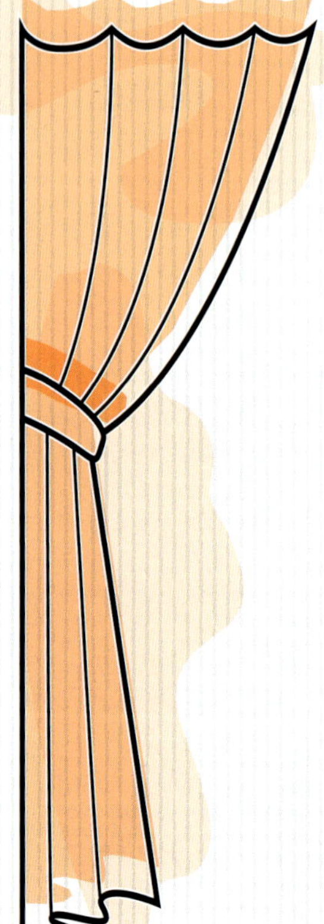

THEATER SETS

Theater designers are in charge of the sets and costumes for plays and musicals. Each play may need very different sets, for example creating the impression of an intimate room or a vast landscape on stage. Designers produce drawings and models of their ideas before making the full-sized set. They also need to be on hand during rehearsals for any changes that the director wants to make.

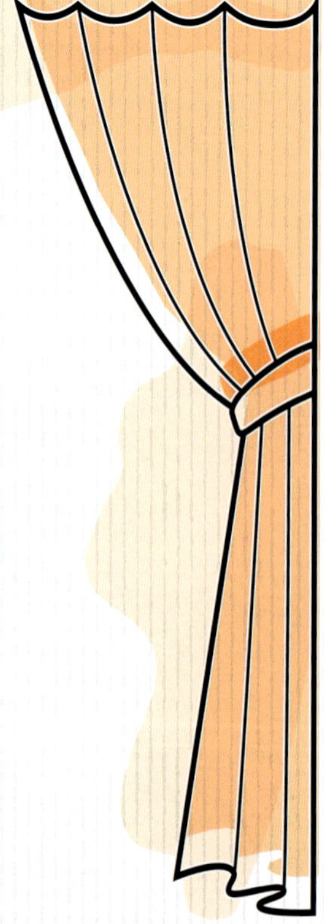

STEAM STAR:
HEIDI ETTINGER
(1951-)

American theater designer Heidi Ettinger made her name designing the sets for a series of hit shows on Broadway in New York. Ettinger is known for creating sets in many different styles, including an award-winning design for *Big River*, a musical based on the Mark Twain novel *Adventures of Huckleberry Finn*.

SCENIC ARTIST

Scenic artists put the painting and sculpture skills that they learned in art school to use by building the props for sets. One week you may be painting an abstract landscape to go at the back of a theater set. The next week, you may be building a realistic landscape in an animal enclosure for a zoo! Scenic artists need to be practical and flexible to help their clients realize their visions.

Special effects artist

Do you spend hours designing ghoulish outfits and makeup for Halloween? You might love creating special effects for films. Working on set doing specialist makeup on actors, or on computer screens long after a film has been shot, special effects artists let their creativity run wild to create weird and wonderful scenes.

COMPUTER EFFECTS

For today's big-budget films, artists create most of the special effects using computer-generated imagery (CGI). These are effects, such as explosions, that are added to the film after it has been shot. In many films, the action is shot in front of blank green screens and the background is added later using CGI. Artists working in CGI combine great computer and technical skills with flair and imagination.

PROSTHETIC MAKEUP

A makeup artist reapplies makeup to an actor on set.

Makeup artists transform actors into a variety of monsters using prosthetics. These are masks or artificial body parts that have been sculpted out of materials such as latex. Prosthetic makeup can turn an actor into anything from an ape to a zombie. In modern films, prosthetic makeup is often combined with CGI to create truly outlandish fiends.

STEAM STAR: RICK BAKER (1950-)

American makeup artist Rick Baker made gory effects for horror and sci-fi films, such as *Men in Black* and *Planet of the Apes*. He specialized in using prosthetic makeup to create ghouls, memorably turning pop star Michael Jackson into a werewolf for the music video *Thriller*. In a 50-year career, Baker won a record seven Best Makeup Oscars before retiring in 2017.

Behind the scenes: Film set

On set, a team of artists and craftspeople form a film's art department, which is responsible for creating the fictional worlds the films are set in. These might be magical fantasy worlds or accurate reconstructions of historical settings. On big-budget productions, an art department may employ hundreds of people, working in a wide variety of roles.

ART DIRECTOR

Art directors are in overall charge of the art department. They are project managers, liaising with directors and production designers during filming, who in turn will instruct their teams. Art directors need to make sure that the right teams are in place and that they are doing exactly what the director wants them to do—mistakes cause delays, and delays in filming can cost thousands of dollars a day.

Film crews can include a large number of people.

Construction crews may have to adjust a set during filming.

BUILDING SETS

Construction crews are responsible for building sets. They include scenic artists and prop-makers, working alongside carpenters, electricians, plasterers, and painters. The construction crews work closely with the camera and lighting crews to achieve the right overall atmosphere for the film. For instance, the director may have asked for a dark, menacing street or a colorful landscape.

LOCATIONS AND PROPS

As well as building sets, members of the art department need to check out locations for filming. These might be grand mansions, city streets, or remote mountains. The team needs to negotiate a price and permission to film. Production buyers source props for the films, scouring shops and markets for just the right pieces. Anything that can't be bought will need to be made from scratch. Artists in the art department provide craftspeople with detailed instructions and drawings to guide them in making each prop.

The set of a *Star Wars* film in Tunisia

Interior designer

Do you insist on having the decor in your bedroom exactly how you want it? Interior designers have strong opinions on how rooms look. They model rooms and other indoor spaces, including private houses, workplaces, and public spaces. They decide on color schemes, furniture, and lighting. You'll need a flair for color combinations and to know how to get the most out of any space.

HEALTHY SPACES

Large companies employ interior designers to create happy and productive workplaces. Having technical know-how in other areas, such as building regulations, psychology, and ergonomics—the study of how people work—would be a real advantage. The goal is to produce beautiful, healthy, eco-friendly environments for people to work in and do it all within a budget!

EXHIBITION SPACES

As well as shaping living and working environments, interior designers are employed by museums and galleries to design exhibition spaces. They arrange the exhibits to give visitors a pleasurable and easy path around the space. Interior designers work closely with curators and researchers to understand the needs of an exhibition, sketching out their ideas before putting them in place.

STEAM STAR: PHILIPPE STARCK (1949-)

French designer Philippe Starck has worked in a wide range of design fields, including furniture, product, and interior design. He has designed the interiors of world-renowned hotels, exclusive restaurants, and even luxury yachts. However, Starck does not just design for the rich and famous. He has created ranges of stylish low-cost furniture and developed affordable wooden eco-houses that consume just one-third of the energy of a traditional house.

Stylist

Do you love flicking through glossy magazines or browsing them online? The food, clothes, and other products in the photos have all been made to look their very best by a stylist. As a stylist, it is your job to choose the items to be featured, selecting objects that show off the latest trends. You'll be out on photo shoots for much of the day, coordinating with the photographer to create images for the magazine.

CLOTHES STYLIST

Do you have a passion for clothes? Fashion stylists coordinate outfits from a selection of clothing and accessories. They may dress mannequins for shop displays or coordinate photo shoots for fashion magazines. A fashion stylist can also help individual customers select the clothes that suit their body shape. Celebrity stylists choose the outfits for famous actors to wear to film premieres or TV appearances.

STEAM STAR: CHERYL KONTEH

British stylist Cheryl Konteh started her career at a national newspaper magazine, but soon moved on to more glamorous work. She discovered that she had a flair for fashion and now she travels the world styling the looks of famous actors. Today, Konteh dresses some of the biggest names in Hollywood, including Idris Elba, Kate Winslet, and Brad Pitt. The next time you watch the Oscars on TV, you will see a host of stars who have been dressed by Cheryl Konteh.

Film star Kate Winslet wears an outfit styled by Konteh.

STYLING FOOD

Food stylists create appealing displays of food for magazines and cookbooks that make you want to lick the page! As a food stylist, you need to love to cook—everything from pizza to pastries. As well as following the recipes perfectly, you need to arrange all the ingredients on the plate to make them look their best. Food stylists have a few sneaky tricks up their sleeve, such as using sprays and glazes to make the food look vibrant and appetizing.

Fashion designer

Do you go into clothes shops to check out the fabrics and construction of eye-catching designs? You could turn your obsession into a career in fashion design. With an eye for color and shape, you will also need hands-on practical skills, such as pattern-cutting and sewing, to turn sketches on a page into the finished garment. One day, people on the red carpet could be trying on your designs.

HAUTE COUTURE

Haute couture (which is French for "high fashion") is the cutting edge of the fashion industry. Top designers make haute couture clothes for very exclusive clients, designing individual items to fit the client's body perfectly. Every piece is made by hand, using only the finest materials. Fashion houses present haute couture collections at fashion shows. The clothes are often daring and unusual and create trends that are later followed by other clothing companies.

STEAM STAR: OZWALD BOATENG (1967-)

British fashion designer Ozwald Boateng is famed for making sharp, stylish suits for men. Working from his London base, Boateng and a team of skilled tailors create made-to-measure suits cut from scratch. Boateng has broken many boundaries in the fashion industry, bringing haute couture glamour into traditional menswear. In 1994, he made history as the first men's tailor to present a catwalk show at Paris Fashion Week.

MAIN STREET DESIGN

Teams of fashion designers develop ready-to-wear clothing ranges for retail stores and online shops. Often inspired by haute couture designs, the teams take the design process from the initial ideas right through to mass production. They need to keep a close eye on the latest trends and they also need to work on very tight deadlines—every new season demands a fresh new range of clothes.

Photographer

Are you always taking photographs with your phone? Do you have a great eye for the right shot? There are lots of ways you can turn a passion for photography into a career. You could work in fashion, sports, wildlife, or portrait photography, or photojournalism. Photographers normally specialize in one or two fields of photography and become experts at capturing the best images.

ON THE STREET

Urban photographers specialize in taking images of life in towns and cities. They may record gritty scenes of urban decay or poverty as part of a project, or take images of everyday events, but from different and interesting angles. Whatever they do choose to show, they need to be highly skilled photographers and ready at a moment's notice, as the perfect picture can appear (and disappear!) in a heartbeat.

WILDLIFE PHOTOGRAPHY

Wildlife photographers take photos of creatures in their natural habitats. They are intrepid explorers and often undertake arduous journeys to dangerous places. Photographers use all kinds of technology to capture the secret lives of animals, including hidden cameras that are triggered when an animal walks by. You'll need patience for this job. Wildlife photographers may wait for weeks or even months to capture a single image, such as the moment a bear emerges from her den with her cubs.

Photographing a hummingbird in flight takes skill and patience.

STEAM STAR: DOROTHEA LANGE (1895–1965)

Dorothea Lange on location in 1936

Photojournalists tell stories with pictures. American photographer Dorothea Lange documented the struggles of the poor and disadvantaged in the United States. She photographed migrant workers during the Great Depression of the 1930s. Later she made a record of the lives of Japanese-American families who were held in prison in the United States during the Second World War (1939–1945). Lange's photographs have since become some of the most recognizable images of that era.

Behind the scenes: Fashion shoot

A fashion shoot involves a team of creative people. In addition to the photographer and the models, a stylist (see pages 16–17) looks after the clothes and makes sure they are being worn properly, while hairdressers and makeup artists are on hand throughout the day to ensure the models look their best. A fashion shoot can happen anywhere! It might take place in a studio or on location in streets, parks, or historic buildings.

IN THE STUDIO

The photographer can control every aspect of the shoot when it is in a studio. Models stand in front of powerful lights that have filters to change the mood, while special effects, such as dry ice, can be introduced to the shoot to create different atmospheres. The photographer will take shots from all kinds of angles as the model adopts a variety of poses.

A model and a photographer at a fashion shoot in a studio setting

Location shoots can involve the photographer working on their own or as part of a bigger team of stylists and assistants.

ON LOCATION

On location, the photographer has to rely on natural light and has much less control of the environment. This leaves lots of room for the unexpected to happen. Some of the best shots can be the result of a total accident, such as a gust of wind blowing the model's hair out at a dramatic angle.

AFTER THE SHOOT

While the models and stylists have finished their work at the end of the shoot, the photographer still has plenty more to do. Together with a production director, they select the best images from hundreds or even thousands of different shots. They then work on the images they have selected on a computer, using a photo editing program. The color balance and contrast of the images are adjusted, while small imperfections in the clothing or background can be smoothed over.

A photographer digitally edits a photograph.

Landscape architect

Do you love helping out in the garden, digging the soil and planting seeds? Landscape architects design green spaces for plants and wildlife that make towns and cities better places in which to live. Working on public parks, housing developments, or wildlife conservation areas, you'll be protecting the environment and improving people's lives.

IMPROVING CITIES

New developments in urban areas need to be eco-friendly. This means that they must have clean air and keep energy use to a minimum. Landscape architects work with town planners to create housing that provide every resident with access to green spaces. These include places for the community to come together and recycle their waste, such as city farms that turn food leftovers into compost for crops.

Modern cities combine built-up areas with open spaces.

STEAM STAR:
ANDRÉ LE NÔTRE
(1613–1700)

French landscape architect André Le Nôtre was the head gardener for King Louis XIV (1638–1715). His best-known creation is the garden at the Palace of Versailles, just outside Paris. It is a stunning example of a French formal garden, featuring sharp geometric shapes and precisely trimmed hedges. Today, Le Nôtre's garden is one of the most popular tourist destinations in France, attracting more than 6 million visitors every year.

A portrait of famed landscape architect, André Le Nôtre

SHOW GARDENS

Each year, some of the best landscape architects in the world are invited to create a show garden for the Chelsea Flower Show in London, England. The gardens might include fountains, wooden structures, or sculptures. One year, an entrant even built a working water wheel! Central to every garden is the stunning selection of plants and flowers. The show gardens are judged by a panel of experts and one garden is declared "Best in Show."

A plant wall at the Chelsea Flower Show in London

Jewelry Designer

Do you love making accessories? Jewelry designers come up with new designs and many make their own pieces in a workshop. You'll need lots of practical skills to work with precious stones and metals, and you'll need an eye for detail. To be a great jewelry designer, you need to be a perfectionist!

CREATING THE DESIGN

Designers often come up with their initial designs in a sketchbook, but the best way to sell your ideas is to show them in 3D. When making jewelery for mass production, designers create images of the designs on a computer, using software that can rotate the design to any angle. Some designers create one-off pieces or collections that they sell themselves. Displaying your work in public is a great way to promote yourself—a successful show can lead to lots of new commissions.

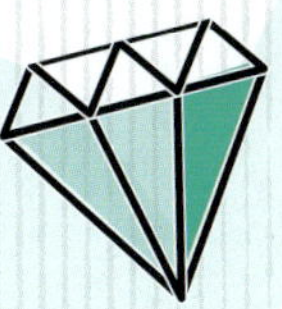

MAKING THE PIECE

Creating a fine piece of jewelry, such as a diamond ring, takes a lot of work. The first stage is called mounting. This involves shaping a precious metal, such as gold or silver, to create the ring, adding the section that secures the stone, and any decorative patterns. Next, the diamond needs to be set in place. This involves very intricate work, such as removing tiny slithers of metal. Finally, the whole piece is polished to make it look its best and any letters or inscriptions on the inside of the ring are engraved by hand.

STEAM STAR: KIM POOR (1952–)

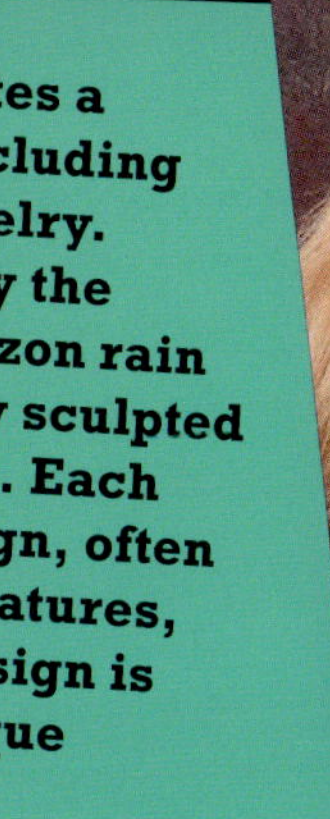

Brazilian artist Kim Poor creates a wide range of artistic work, including paintings, sculptures, and jewelry. Much of her work is inspired by the people and animals of the Amazon rain forest. Poor makes individually sculpted rings, necklaces, and brooches. Each piece features an intricate design, often incorporating mythological creatures, such as a winged angel. The design is created by hand using a technique called chasing.

Product designer

If you look around a room, most of the things you see, from your chair to the light you are reading with, had to be designed. Product designers combine design skills with technical knowledge to create products that look good and perform their function superbly. These might be furniture, new ranges of cutlery, or specialist medical or electronics equipment.

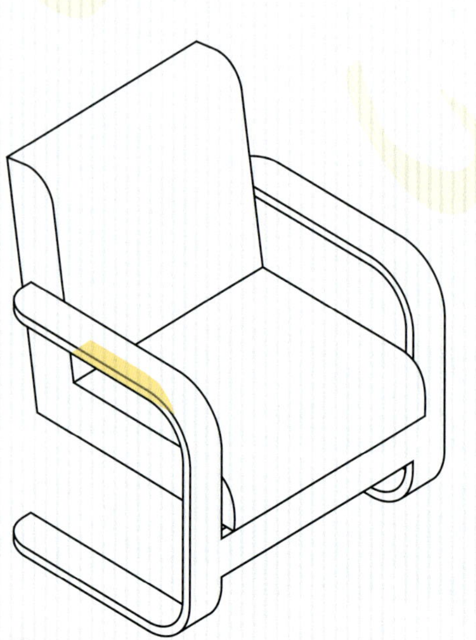

FURNITURE DESIGNER

Furniture designers create new designs for mass-produced items, furniture made in small quantities, or one-off pieces. Designers take their ideas from an initial sketch to make test models before their designs go into production. As well as design skills, you'll need lots of technical know-how about how furniture is made and the qualities of different materials. Many furniture designers start their careers as apprentices, learning the craft of furniture-making before they turn their hand to design.

STEAM STARS: ERWAN (1976-) AND RONAN (1971-) BOUROULLEC

French brothers Erwan (left) and Ronan Bouroullec (right) have won multiple awards for their elegant modern furniture. They often incorporate surprising shapes into their designs, which include wavy-edged interlocking ceramic vases and a table with a bowl molded into it. By doing this, the Bouroullecs hope to encourage their customers to think creatively, finding new uses for their furniture that the designers hadn't thought of. In addition to furniture, the brothers are also noted for their minimalist lighting designs.

INDUSTRIAL DESIGNER

Industrial designers work on products that are mass-produced in factories. In addition to designing the item, an industrial designer must come up with a production process that is cost-effective. One of today's biggest challenges involves creating green production processes that reduce waste and energy use and employ more sustainable materials. In this way, industrial design provides a link between science and creativity.

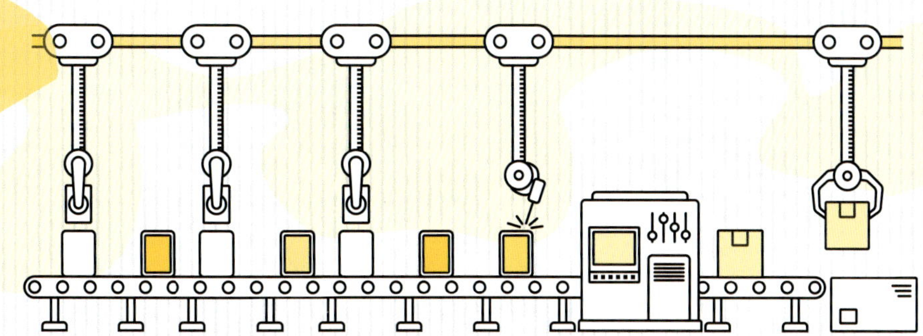

Behind the scenes: Herman Miller

U.S. manufacturer Herman Miller makes furniture for offices and the home. The company is known for its innovative, stylish ranges that have changed the way people work by rearranging office spaces. Herman Miller's factory has manufactured the designs of many famous furniture designers.

DESIGN CLASSIC

Herman Miller's best-selling piece of furniture is an office chair called the Aeron Chair, which was first made in 1992. The fully adjustable revolving chair is made from recycled materials and can be recycled itself when it reaches the end of its life. The company makes more than 1 million Aeron Chairs each year in its factory, which can put together a whole chair in just 21 seconds!

The Aeron Chair

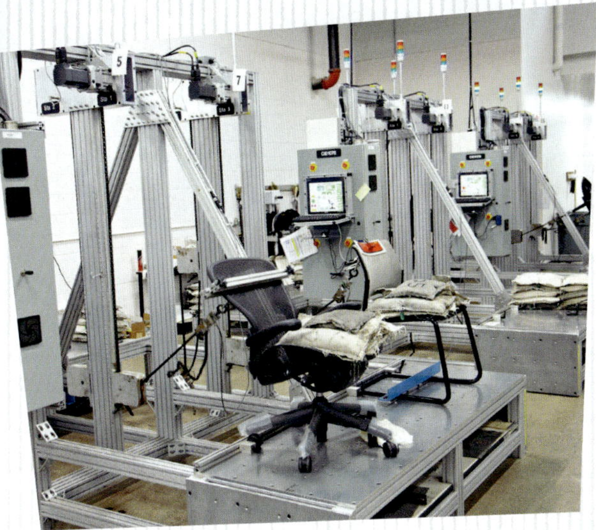

Herman Miller's testing facility

TESTED TO DESTRUCTION

In a special testing laboratory, Herman Miller puts furniture through a rigorous set of tests to ensure it is worthy of the company's 12-year guarantee. An office chair might receive up to 1 million different movements to test the weight it can support and to make sure the materials it is made from are up to a high standard.

ART AND SCIENCE

It takes the design team at Herman Miller up to three years to develop a new piece of furniture. The designs need to look good, feel good, and be easy to manufacture. The designers take advice from a range of experts, including doctors and psychologists, to create furniture that keeps people happy and healthy, whether they are at work or at home.

Herman Miller designers study models of future chair designs

Graphic designer

Do you make collages or collect your favorite images in a scrapbook? Graphic designers put their eye for a great image to use in a range of illustrated works, including books, magazines, posters, websites, film posters, and album covers. They combine images with words to create fantastic, eye-catching, informative designs.

WORDS AND IMAGES

For magazines, newspapers, and other publications, graphic designers work with both images and words. They select the fonts, colors, and size of the typeface, and place text on or around the images. You'll often need to get creative to make new images such as infographics—fun ways of visually displaying information in the form of graphs and diagrams. Many designers work for several different publications, so you will work in many different styles.

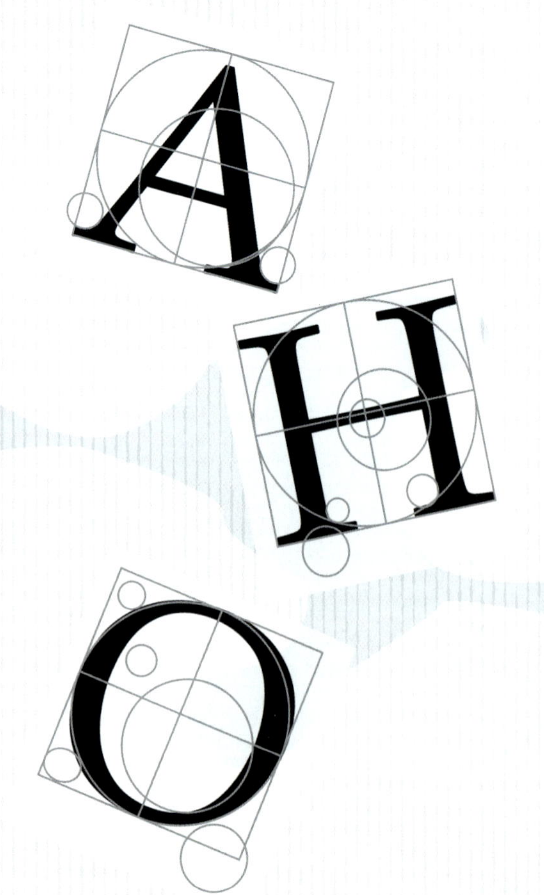

STEAM STAR: CAROLYN DAVIDSON (1941-)

American graphic designer Carolyn Davidson designed the Nike Swoosh, one of the most famous logos in the world. In 1971, Davidson was a student at Portland State University, Oregon, when she was asked to design the logo by Nike founder Phil Knight. She was paid a fee of just $35 for the job. Later, after Nike had become a successful worldwide company, Knight gave Davidson shares in the company in recognition of the importance of her logo design.

Serena Williams wearing Nike clothing

POSTER DESIGN

As you walk down a city street, you're surrounded by images. These could be huge billboards advertising new goods, such as smartphones, or posters for the latest films or music concerts. These posters were put together by graphic designers. Designing film posters is considered a form of art and the best posters may still be on show decades after they were made. That's a great way to make your name as a graphic designer!

Illustrator

Do you find yourself doodling sketches whenever you have a spare minute? You could turn those doodles into a career as an illustrator. Working by hand or digitally, illustrators put their drawing skills to use producing original artwork for books, magazines, websites, posters, or greeting cards. You'll need to be flexible in your style and able to work to a client's needs.

A technical drawing of a mechanical device

TECHNICAL ILLUSTRATOR

Technical illustrators produce highly detailed images to show how things work. These might be cross-sections of body parts for medical journals or step-by-step diagrams for instruction manuals. Technical illustrators work from very precise instructions to make accurate images that are easy to understand. You'll often need detailed knowledge of the subject area and many technical illustrators specialize in one subject, such as medicine, botany, or engineering.

ILLUSTRATED FICTION

Freed from the constraints of technical illustration, an artist's imagination can run wild when they are illustrating fiction. Storybooks for young children are usually illustrated, with just a few words on each page to help tell the story. Graphic novels are books written in comic-strip style, with dialogue appearing in speech bubbles. Graphic novels may be written for children or adults.

STEAM STAR: AXEL SCHEFFLER (1957-)

German illustrator Axel Scheffler works with authors to make illustrated fiction for children. He has collaborated with British author Julia Donaldson on a number of books, including *The Gruffalo*, an international best seller about a cunning mouse who fools a giant creature called a gruffalo on a walk in the woods.

Art director

Are there magazines you pick up simply because you love their style? Art directors create the visual style for magazines, books, or advertising campaigns. Working with writers, graphic designers, stylists, and photographers, the art director is in charge of signing off the final designs before they go to print.

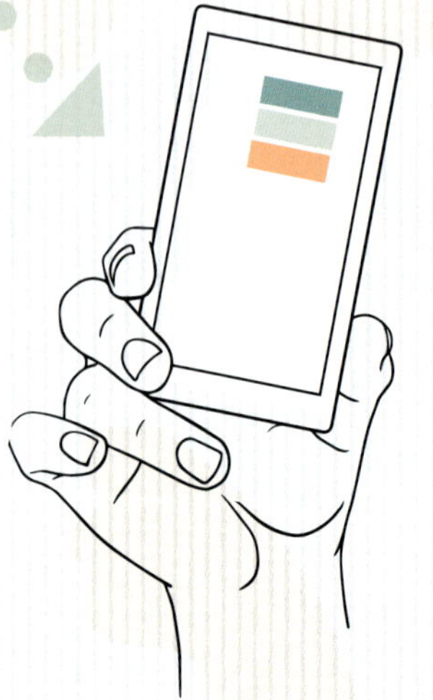

MODERN MEDIA

Today's media are normally produced for a range of platforms. A magazine doesn't just appear in print. Art directors must make sure their designs look just as good on a tablet or a smartphone as they do on a printed page. They also need to engage with social media, maintaining a lively online presence to make sure their magazine is seen by as many people as possible.

ADVERTISING

In advertising, the art director works closely with copywriters to come up with striking and memorable images and catchphrases for a wide range of media. An advertising campaign might include posters, TV ads, and webpages. The art director creates a memorable look to go across the whole campaign. They need a wide range of skills as they may be laying out a poster design one day and directing a photo shoot the next.

STEAM STAR: NEVILLE BRODY (1957-)

British graphic designer Neville Brody made his name as art director for the music and style magazine *The Face*. He created visually striking layouts in which the photos took center stage. Brody's work helped change the way magazines are laid out, making them much more image-conscious. Today, he runs an international design company, developing fresh new looks for a variety of companies, newspapers, and magazines.

Behind the scenes:
Designing a brand

A company's brand is its recognizable public image. Companies spend a lot of money developing and protecting their brand. They employ advertising agencies to come up with new ideas for promoting the brand. Once they have created a recognizable logo, the companies seek to give the logo positive exposure. They often do this by sponsoring sports, theater, or other cultural events.

Advertising in New York's Times Square means millions will see your brand every day.

CREATING A BRAND

Developing a trusted brand is crucial for a company's success, creating confidence in their products. Brand designers work on all aspects of a company's public face, from the look and message of advertising campaigns to the sponsorship of public events. An overall brand manager coordinates each aspect of the brand, making sure every detail is correct—down to using exactly the right font in the ads.

CLEVER BRANDING

Advertising professionals speak of Volkswagen's 1960 advertising campaign as one of the best ever. Most Americans at the time liked big powerful cars. Volkswagen was selling the compact Beetle and made a virtue of its size in ads that made the car appear tiny, alongside the slogan "Think small." Within a few years, the Beetle, or Bug as it was called in the United States, had become the most popular imported car in the country. Small cars were cool!

Volkswagen Beetle

MERCHANDISING

Companies often promote their brands by creating a range of merchandise that carries their company logo. This might include anything from hats and T-shirts to notebooks or USB drives. Companies often pay large sums of money to place their merchandise at big public events, such as a soccer World Cup. But it needs to be good quality stuff, otherwise customers will associate the brand with something that doesn't work!

Advertising surrounds fields at most major sporting events.

Fine artist

Do you love painting pictures and showing them off to your friends and family? Fine artists create original works of art, such as paintings and sculptures, which can be sold to private collectors or displayed in art galleries. You'll need to be really determined to make it as a fine artist as it can be hard to make a living. Many fine artists teach or work in galleries to support their fine art careers.

The moving *Man and Woman* statue in Batumi, Georgia

PUBLIC ART

Sculptors are often commissioned to create a work to be displayed in a particular public place, such as a square or a park. These could be sculptures of a famous person or to commemorate famous events. Sometimes the sculptures are just intended to provide some fun or amazement. In 2007, Georgian artist Tamara Kvesitadze created a moving sculpture of a man and woman. The slices of each figure pass through each other, with the figures emerging intact again on the other side.

SHOWING YOUR WORK

Once you have made a collection of works, it is time to put on a show. Fine artists display their latest collections in galleries, either in solo shows or with a group of artists. Many artists get great satisfaction from showing their work and selling their pieces. A lucky few will be featured in the media or have their work bought by a famous museum. If they become well known, they will sell more of their work and command much higher prices.

STEAM STAR: GONÇALO MABUNDA (1975-)

Mozambican artist and peace activist Gonçalo Mabunda creates sculptures out of guns, rockets, and bombs that were used during Mozambique's 16-year civil war. Mabunda's art has been displayed at museums around the world. He works in partnership with the organization African Artists for Development, which encourages artists to get involved in community projects.

Mabunda's sculpture *A Throne for Two Kings*

Behind the scenes: Restoring *The Night Watch*

Conservation departments in art galleries conserve and restore works of art. In a special project at the Rijksmuseum in Amsterdam, The Netherlands, a painting called *The Night Watch* is being restored by a team of experts in full view of the public. The team includes scientists, art historians, and specialist restorers. You can tune in and watch their progress live on the internet. The restoration is expected to take several years to complete.

THE PAINTING

The Night Watch is the Rijksmuseum's most prized possession. Painted in 1642 by Rembrandt van Rijn (1606–1669), it is a huge canvas—more than 13 feet (4 m) wide and 9.8 feet (3 m) high—depicting a group of city militiamen walking through a crowd. *The Night Watch* is famed for its use of light and shadow, contrasting brightly lit figures with a menacingly dark background, a technique called tenebrism. The restoration is being carried out because parts of the painting's background have faded.

***The Night Watch* by Rembrandt**

X-RAY SCAN

Working inside a protective glass case, the experts will first scan the whole painting inch by inch using a special machine called an X-ray fluorescence scanner. The machine uses high-energy X-rays to identify the chemical elements in the paint, such as iron, potassium, or cobalt. In total, 56 different scans will be carried out to fully analyze every layer of paint.

Conservation artists may have to remove old, damaged paint before replacing it.

MATCHING THE COLORS

Once the scanning and analysis are complete, the restorers will know exactly how Rembrandt made each of his colors. They plan to recreate Rembrandt's paints in order to carry out the restoration using authentic methods. For instance, they know that, for his blue paint, Rembrandt used cobalt, which he ground from smalt—a kind of powdered glass.

Smalt was used to make bottles and glasses and could be ground up to make cobalt pigment.

Art therapist

Does creating art make you feel good? Art therapists tap into the healing power of art to help people feel better about themselves. They work with children or adults, using art to help them express their emotions and explore their innermost fears. Art therapists may be artists who have trained in psychology or nurses or teachers who have trained in art.

HEALTH SERVICES

The term "art therapy" was coined by British artist Adrian Hill in 1942, who discovered the benefits of making art for patients who were recovering from tuberculosis. At first, art therapists like Hill were self-taught, but today art therapists study the subject at school, learning psychotherapy techniques. Health services around the world employ art therapists to help patients with a wide range of difficulties, including mentally ill people, people with learning disabilities, and people with chronic illnesses.

OUTSIDER ART

While art therapy is focused on helping people feel better, it can also produce some amazing works of art. The term "outsider art" refers to art made by people with no artistic training. Many outsider artists first start making art in art therapy classes. Autistic British artist Stephen Wiltshire started drawing before he had learned to talk, and his first word was "paper." Today, he has his own gallery, displaying his incredibly detailed drawings. He is able to draw an entire cityscape from memory after a single helicopter ride over the area.

British artist Stephen Wiltshire

STEAM STAR: EDWARD ADAMSON (1911–1996)

Edward Adamson was the first artist to be employed by the UK National Health Service, working with patients in Netherne psychiatric hospital from the 1940s to the 1990s. Adamson helped the patients express themselves in art works that were later exhibited to the public in group shows. In 1984, he wrote an influential book about his work called *Art as Healing*. His pioneering work helped win funding for many other art therapy projects.

Glossary

animation
the joining together of a series of pictures to create the effect of a moving image

app
short for "application," a computer program that does a particular job (such as making digital art)

apprentice
a person who works for a skilled tradesperson, often for low wages, in order to learn the trade

autism
a condition that causes difficulties in learning how to communicate with others and behave in social situations

botany
the study of plants

catwalk
a narrow stage at a fashion show, down which models walk. The catwalk allows everybody in the audience to get a close look at the clothes.

ceramics
pots or other items shaped from soft clay that have been baked in a kiln to make them hard

chasing
the creation of a pattern in a sheet of metal by hammering from the reverse side to create a raised design. It is also called repoussage.

chronic illness
a long-term health condition that may not have a cure. Patients with chronic illnesses may become depressed about their condition and can be helped with art therapy.

cobalt
a metallic chemical element that is used to make blue pigments

collage
a piece of art created by pasting different objects next to one another on a flat surface, such as a piece of paper or wood

color theory
the science behind the way we see colors. Color theory explains how to combine colors to create different effects.

commission
an order from a client to do a particular job

conservation area
an area of special interest that is protected. It may be countryside with unique wildlife or an urban zone with historic buildings.

copywriter
the person who writes the text to go alongside images in advertising or other publicity material

curator
the person in charge of a particular collection in a museum or a gallery

ergonomics
the study of how people work and how to design a work environment

formal garden
a garden in which the plants have all been specially chosen and are trimmed to create geometric shapes

geometric shapes
shapes, such as circles, squares, triangles, and hexagons, that are created according to certain mathematical rules

glaze
a treatment applied to items of food, ceramics, and other materials to make their surfaces smooth and shiny

Great Depression
a period during the 1930s during which many parts of the world experienced economic hardship, with high unemployment and widespread hunger

infographic
a visual way of showing information that makes it easy to understand

logo
a symbol or design that instantly identifies a company or organization

merchandise
goods that have been made to be bought and sold

minimalist
a style in art, design, or music that has deliberately been kept simple

photojournalist
a photographer who tells news stories by taking a series of photos

pigment
a substance with a particular color. Pigments are often made in powder form.

precious metal
a metal that is only found on Earth in small quantities and that is highly valued for its chemical properties

prosthetic
an artificial body part, such as an arm or a foot

psychiatric hospital
a hospital that cares for patients suffering from mental illness

psychology
the scientific study of the human mind and the ways in which humans behave in different situations

psychotherapy
also called "talking therapy," treatment of mental illnesses using psychological methods rather than medical means, such as drugs

recycling
turning waste materials into useful new things

restoration
returning an old object, such as an artwork, to its original condition

sculpture
a three-dimensional work of art

set
a specially created scene that has been designed for a film or a play

sustainability
a way of creating human development that meets our needs for today without destroying resources that we will need in the future

tailor
a person who designs and makes clothing for men, such as suits

tenebrism
a technique in painting in which areas of shadow are contrasted with brightly colored areas to create dramatic effects

tuberculosis
an infectious disease—usually of the lungs—that is caused by bacteria

X-rays
a form of high-energy radiation that can be used to look inside bodies or underneath layers of paint in an artwork

Index

Adamson, Edward 45
advertising 37, 38, 39
Aeron Chair 30
ancient artists 4
animators 6–7
art college 5
art directors 12, 36–37
art therapists 44–45

Baker, Rick 11
Boateng, Ozwald 19
book illustrators 35
Bouroullec, Erwan and Ronan 29
brand designers 38–39
Brody, Neville 37

celebrity stylists 16
computer-generated imagery (CGI) 10
conservation artists 42–43
construction crews 13

Davidson, Carolyn 33

Ettinger, Heidi 9
exhibition spaces 15

fashion designers 18–19
fashion shoots 22–23
fashion stylists 16, 17, 22
film sets 12–13
fine artists 40–41
food stylists 17
furniture designers 28, 29, 30–31

graphic designers 32–33, 36, 37
graphic novels 35

haute couture 18, 19
Hill, Adrian 44

illustrators 34–35
industrial designers 29
infographics 32
interior designers 14–15

jewelry designers 26–27

Konteh, Cheryl 17

landscape architects 24–25
Lange, Dorothea 21
Le Nôtre, André 25
location scouts 13

Mabunda, Gonçalo 41
makeup artists 11, 22
merchandising 39
Miller, Herman 30–31
Miyazaki, Hayao 7

Night Watch, The (Rembrandt) 42–43
Nike Swoosh 33

outsider artists 45

photographers 20–23, 36
photojournalists 21
Poor, Kim 27
poster designers 33
practical skills 5
product designers 28–31
production buyers 13
prop-makers 13
prosthetic makeup 11

scenic artists 9, 13
Scheffler, Axel 35
sculptors 40, 41
set designers 8–9
special effects artists 10–11
Starck, Philippe 15
storyboard artists 6
stylists 16–17, 22, 23, 36

technical illustrators 34

urban photographers 20

wildlife photographers 21
Wiltshire, Stephen 45

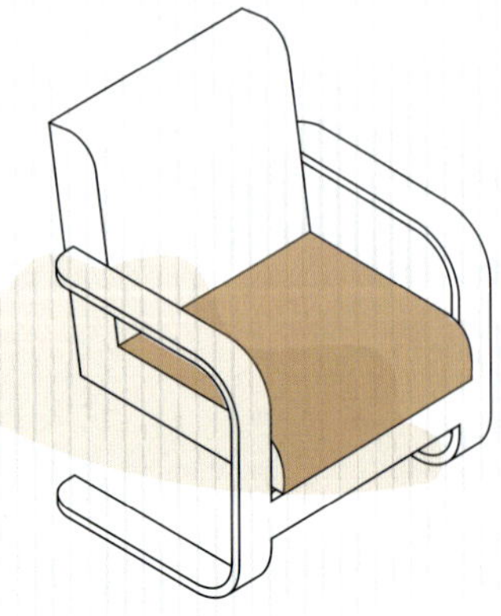